There is Only One Truth

Trevor David Honour

The Vagabond Poet

Watching the Pacific roll in from a Costa Rican Beach Bar

Three weeks after my 17th birthday, I threw two shirts and a pair of pants into a canvas backpack, hitchhiked 1500 miles to the west coast and made my home in the back of a deserted 1956 Oldsmobile station wagon.... that was 1964.... the journey had begun.... and it has been a journey of wits, intrigue, and adventure.

The road has always been my home. From building a house above the Arctic circle, to teaching firefighting in the British West Indies, it has been a wild ride. I have sailed the Caribbean and muddled and fumbled my way through cross country tours with some of the great musicians of our time. All through this time I have recorded the inner fire in verse and rhyme.

Table of Contents

The function of the artist is to disturb. His duty is to arouse the sleepers, to shake the complacent pillars of the world. He is the agitator, a disturber of the peace-- quick, impatient, positive, restless and disquieting.
He is the creative spirit working in the soul of man

Norman Bethdune

Chapter One

Reflections From the Road

GYPSY SOUL

Painted wagons circled, near the river, by the glen
Twilight is upon us and our journey soon begins.
The old man and the trail boss, scout the border line,
The guards along the border will be gone by first light
The old man tells the trail boss, the moon is full tonight
Rises from the mountains, as the north-star drifts from sight.

I've always liked to travel, I've always liked to roam
Something about the highway, it's now become my home
And when I'm standing next to you, in silence all alone
I can feel your own affection for the gypsy in your soul

Mother reads the tea leaves, sister does her dance
Father leaves for weeks and returns with gifts and cash
I prepare the wagon for its border crossing ride
And listen to the wisdom, of those we dwell beside
And follow in the footsteps and remember all the tales
For I am only seven, and a gypsy on the trail

We load our painted wagons, and hitch up all our teams
Like our fathers did before us, like we do inside your dreams
We move across the border, as the moon lights up our way
And journey to our resting place, a thousand miles away
We live within the moment and repeat the ancient times
Caught by superstition, and the creed to the gypsy life.

We have no need for borders, or those patriotic fools
That cling to others judgment and their tax collecting rules
Cursed by those that pass us, for they do not understand
The guiding light within us, has burned for countless times
Ancestors have shown us, the world that lives by chance
Recognized by kindred souls affording just a glance

I've always liked to travel, I've always liked to roam
Living in the refection, of the gypsy in my soul
And when I'm standing next to you, in silence all alone
I can feel your own affection for the gypsy in your soul
It comes from deep within you like a well spring flow
You always could connect with it, the gypsy in your soul

Ever stopped to wonder, is there gypsy in your soul
Do your dreams cry out to meet you, where the wagons roll
Do you ponder on the moment, and follow moments rule
And allow yourself to follow, the lonely mystic road
It comes from deep within you, like a well spring flow
You always could connect with it, the gypsy in your soul

And when I'm standing next to you, in silence all alone
I can feel your own affection for the gypsy in your soul
It comes from deep within you, like a well spring flow
You always could connect with it, the gypsy in your soul

Grey Hair Blues

It's been six long years since Jack passed away,
Seems like he's still living large,
His chair is still there, found his slippers today,
Behind that Christmas box in the garage.

The dull ache of alone, is always right there,
It just never goes too far away
And it's just inner pride, and the joy to survive,
That helps her to face a new day.

From content and smiling to deep despair,
When that part of your life it has gone
With no one right there, to comfort and care,
It's a hush that calls to us all

Plans for the future, are all put to rest
When that sudden silence does call
You slip from happy to deep despair,
To the sound of the clock on the wall

Sally and Sue, know just what to do,
Now that they are best friends
They both lost their spouse, and live in the house
That their husbands had built them by hand

Swim club and bingo on Monday and Wednesday,
The Friday night social brings cheers
But early on Sunday when the hour is quiet,
There's time for reflection and tears

If fate will guide you to the right moment,
And all of your friends are right here
Then we can say at some future day,
We face our soul without fear

Badger's Drift

A town called Badgers Drift, in the English country side
I think I'd like to go there and spend a little time
Something that appeals to me, somewhere on my own
In a foreign little town, where I'm not even known

I hide there in the shadows, watch the world go by
And listen to the insanity, of who and what and why
Puppets of some inner cause, their actions on display
Prove their worth to someone else, before they walk away.

Sometimes when the air goes still, before a gentle breeze
I have an inspiration, that sets me weak around my knees
The vibe of akashic wisdom, through the actions that I see
It is the inspiration, removed from hate or greed.

I always could relate to it, the Buddha that's within
But sometimes I ignore him, just before I sin
And set up situations, that only I will win
And I run wild with a stallion's pride, and curse myself again.

Sons of Ibuprofen

We are the Sons of Ibuprofen, and finally earned the right
To do just what we want, if we can sleep through the night
Forget about the aches and pains, take two to make it right
And march on to our eternity, inside the zoo of life.

First light through the palm tree, another day begins
Wonder what I'll do today, got to make some plans
Maybe water Zumba, and splash around all day
Maybe I'll just ride my bike, and wave as I ride by

Some just have an attitude, from some past event or day
I just kinda smile at them, then be on my way
To some eventful place and laugh the day away
Just take two before your through, or there's hell to pay.

Time Traveler

I just stepped over a borderline; watching the locals move
To the rhythm of their lifestyles not wanting to intrude
I slip amongst the shadows, watching from afar
Learn the rules, play the fools, watch for your morning star

Yes, I am a stranger here, although it's now my home
I'm just another face to them, they want to be alone
It takes some getting used to, this chameleon in me
But then, from where they stand, it's the introvert they see

But if you are from somewhere else, need to learn the rules
Every town is different, and every town has fools
Depending on the attitude, the rules they seem to change
It's just the local customs, that you may think are strange

That's the rule that guides their life, their family and home
The rules that guide your life, you always want to roam
You are now the traveler, everything is new
Just you and your horizon, opportunities are few

The sailors Port of Marigot, French West Indies side
Take some special cautions, if you want to stay alive
Sailing on a midnight boat, is not the best of plans
But the cash you make carries on, when you get to land

I once slipped down to Montserrat, a mountain island home
Clouds hang in the forest, you never were alone
A six-foot lizard rustles by, take it in your stride
Hike the volcano mountain, with your trusty guide

A pepper plant refinery, that aroma envelops you
You put off being hungry, nothing you can do
Walk to the sights of a seaside town, two miles ahead of you
Check in to some seaside room and eat some rabbit stew.

Monserrat at carnival, is like no other place
A thousand natives in the street dancing in your face
Best you be color blind, if you want a good time
You are the only white man there, and its island party time

Trying to be normal, in this day and time
Takes some getting used to, like living in a distant time
A chameleon can change his skin and tends to blend right in
And when my time is done, I'll be reborn as a chameleon

Charlie

Charlie the flamingo, is only one foot tall
Made of molded plastic, and travels with our home
Always grabs attention, coyotes leave him alone
Charlie is our mascot, where ever the boondock roams

The boondock is our camper, it tags along behind
And finds itself in wilderness, it's where it comes alive
Propane keeps us warm, solar panels keep us lit
But it's that big black tank onboard, that lets us take a shit.

We are modern adventurers, challenging the wilds
Like we want to domineer, some disobedient child
But take away our comforts and we really do complain
About the inconvenience, with anguish and distain.

Someday when adventure calls, and we head off for the hills
Maybe we will understand the meaning of it all
Every animal and bird agree, and prove it with their flight
Human do not have a clue, about the rights of life.

Charlie has his purpose, it's quite easy to explain
He is the only animal, that does not run away
The fleeting flight of wildlife, when we get too near
Proves to us without a doubt, we've taught them to fear

First light hits the Mountain

First light hits the mountain, and I've been up for hours
A whisper from the mountain Jay, the calling of an owl
Sleep sometimes evades me, and the anger dwells within
Of how you lied to me, and how you could begin
To think I'd be your servant, after everything you did

You thought that you could con, a man for a married life
And just ignore the vow you took, and let him live in strife
And when asked how come, you changed so much
You said we were courting then, so much for your trust
I gave you too much of me, and it all turned into rust

And the child we made is broken, she has turned to dust
And lives alone in solitude, with no one she can trust
And I have lived a life, of anguish and distrust
To anyone who comes near me, for fear it turns to rust.
There is a piece inside my heart, that has been broken off.

Friendships

When a friendship you hold starts to unfold,
And no one is paying it mind

Then one quiet day you both slip away,
And hope they made out just fine

All of the effort and all of the time
To decide on a stranger's true mind

To turn a stranger into a lifelong friend,
Takes trust, ambition, and time.

Going Solo

Searching for some sanity, with this nasty bug around
Think I'll do some camping, and hang on hidden ground
Away from all the multitudes, playing their corporate games
Listen to the wilderness, and watch the songbirds play

Maybe I'll go sailing and live way out on the sea
Away from all this history of mass insanity
I can fish to stay alive it really is a gift
To make a life all by myself, and the wind will set my drift

But vows and obligations, bring me back to earth
Now I fully understand, the net of all my worth
It's not the material things, or toys like giant yachts
It's the ones that touch your soul, in tight emotional knots

Have you ever met someone, that showed their inner soul?
Like it was just an open book, for everyone to hold
Is it just an inner gift, or learned behavior from their life?
The only one that ever knows, is the one who lives inside

Friendships get developed from the first hello
Lifetime partners hold the key to making you grow
Into someone you should be, not what you think or want
It's the potential that they see, not the flaws they flaunt

Going Solo lets you travel, very quick and lean
Adventures hold the key to everything you've seen
But in the quiet hours, when reflections are the norm
You are the only one, who weathered all the storms

No one saw the anguish, the fear or the mistrust
Living in a foreign land, and watch it turn to dust
Fight to end the slavery, that others imposed on you
Living with the stigma, of being a solo fool.

Sneaking over borders, in the dead of night
Sailing through a raging storm, with fear that grips so tight
It's only you that understands, and everyone agrees
That when your Solo travelling, it can be a mystery

It builds the inner strength in you, something that you need
And keeps the senses extra sharp, survival is the key
But in the quiet times, when reflections are the norm
You are the only one, that survived all of those storms.

Life on a Schooner

Just caught sight of Southport light,
hard a-beam Goat Island
Tonight, I'll set the anchor down,
in a Boothbay Harbor town.
Sailing up the coast of Maine,
it's the wind that guides us
One day you set the spinnaker high,
next day the storm jib flies

Living off the coast of Maine,
storm-hooked hidden hideaway
We live a life all by ourselves,
and watch the osprey play
I've grown apart from mainstream life,
set my anchor firmly
Listen to my inner song,
and live by the changing tides.

Took my bride for a ride,
through the Caribbean
Wanted to see what we could see,
that winter had us missing
We anchored in some sandy coves,

deserted islands all in view
Didn't get home till the credit cards,
were two months overdue

Slipped the lines at Browns wharf,
high tide Nassau Harbour
A six-day run on the gulf stream tide,
brings me back to Maine.
Empty suits and bangled boots,
never were appealing
Now I listen to the pulse of life,
and live by the changing tides

Living in some sandy cove,
storm Hooked hidden hideaway
We live a life all by ourselves,
and watch the nature play
I've grown apart from mainstream life,
set my anchor firmly
Listen to my inner song,
and live by the changing tides.

Lonely Hollow Walls

No one stays in touch any more
No one ever calls
I just listen to the empty sound
Of the lonely hollow walls

I am going back to my home town
Been years I am away
I don't know anyone
I'd like to keep it just that way

I could walk down through the riverside park
Look at the house I used to stay
Wonder if they still rent that room
And how much I would pay.

Mother Nature in Her Majesty

Mother nature in her majesty, she already has a plan
To carry on this planet, without the help of man.
In my life I have seen the change, animals have disappeared
The majesty of what I've seen, now brings me to tears
I once ran a trap line, in my younger years
Now I sit and watch anything alive and how it lives in fear.

Redneck fools do not care, social climbers have no time
Shruburb larva have no clue, about this cause of mine
This land is not ours; we just pay the rent
We're using mother nature's gifts, that money's all got spent
Just remember when I leave, I leave without a trace
And hang my head in silence, at the human race.

Month of May

Here we are in the month of May
Looks like it has come to stay
Dandelion blooms have blown away
And the aphids are all here to stay
The clock on the wall it still moves
But my calendar app is stuck in a groove
Time drags on but flowers not bloomed
I can't seem to wait for June
If it wasn't for my garden plots
I would not have to move
I guess it's not hard to make
Couch potato stew.

Outbound Train

You're not bad looking, showing off that twinkle in your eye
Now don't lead me on, why would you even try?
I travel all alone, but I never will fly blind
The only thing that holds me, like a changing tide
I'm a solo traveler, with a married state of mind

The future's never certain, just a simple twist of fate
You can go from all your trinkets, and a pretty front gate
To standing all alone and cold in the pouring rain
And your dreams all fade with a bitter refrain
And you end up like baggage on an outbound train.

You never seem to find, the perfect frame of mind
You just keep drifting, like the changing tide
And the song in your heart hides a distant gain
And your dreams all fade with the falling rain
And you end up like baggage on an outbound train
Your eyes start to wander, in the morning light
From whoever that it was, that you held last night
And you never could stay true to any one man
As you watch his dreams all fade in a bitter refrain
You're just loading his baggage on an outbound train.

Sometimes what it takes, and we all know it's true
You hide your true motives; you end up like a fool
And your heart song dies from the falling rain
And your dreams all fade in a bitter refrain
And you become the baggage on an outbound train.

Sound of a Ricochet

That was the sound of a ricochet,
Another bullet from your soul
It comes from deep within you,
Where no one wants to go
Deep within the inner you,
It's all for you alone
To walk in the halo of a deep dark soul,
Where you alone will go.

Deep within the stillness
In the song of the wilderness
I found an inner strength in me
That no one will contest
I have no need to prove my worth
To any one or thing
I just let the present moment
Listen to the ricochet as it sings

The Poet

Deep inside the city grit, a stranger comes alive
And walks alone in solitude, avoiding city lights
He is not some dark soul with a dark evil intent
He is just a poet, whose life is almost spent

I've always liked to travel, I've always like to roam
The highway is in front of me, the highway is my home.

To be a poet often means, disturbing status quo
What good is poetry, if your subject is all known?
Take a step to the edge of life, then take a final leap
You can dance alone at night, or take it to the street

He hides in quiet solitude, distant from the rest
Remembers the mark he made, before his time was spent
Always travels onward, while travelling inside
Bus stops and hotel rooms, or home at the fireside

I've always liked to travel, I've always like to roam
The highway is in front of me, the highway is my home.

Sometimes when my world gets small, or issues tighten me
I look to the horizon, like I was out at sea
Haul my halyard right in tight, to catch the morning breeze
Then travel on through life, with grace, and poise, and ease

You can't fix Stupid

You can't fix stupid, that is a proven fact
Corona virus came to town, it'll take care of that
So go ahead, leave your face bare
Obviously self-absorbed, obviously you don't care
About the health of all the citizens
That breathe the nearby air

Some day you will wave the flag
And know just what it means
To be a part of community
That looks out for other's needs
But you just don't care, and it's not fair
To anyone that has to breathe your air.

I Gave Up my Life for my Country

I gave my life up for my country
Fate said, it was time for me to go
And now I am the essence of the stillness,
That you feel upon the air, just before a breeze is there,
And for just one brief moment I am here

I gave my Rolex to my gunny
I gave the chief my ruby ring
The squadron has all of my memories
They were just some things, and stuff I could not bring
On my journey back to my home

It's that burning flame within us,
That holds us to this cluttered game of life
And the very thought of letting go
Is nothing more than fear, of ever getting near
To someone who could read your inner soul

We all hide from our existence,
Afraid that we will find that hidden road
That will lead us through the mirror's gaze.
Then you just let go, and project your inner soul
And share it with the world like it's a gift.

I see my country is now divided
The fantasy of left and right is every where
But if you see the depth of what is near you
It was love not hate, that made this country great
Then take my hand and together we move on.

I'm standing in Gods waiting room
A Winterhaven sunny afternoon
I have all my new friends around me
There is so much I want to do, and I want to see it through
This just happened way too soon,

There is so much I want to do, and I want to see it through
This just happened way too soon.

It's not Hard to Give Up

It's not hard to give up, on the one that you love
When their actions are lies and betrayal
And through no fault of your own, everything you own
Is a burden that sets you fragile and frail

Then comes the day, a breeze blows your way
And you just turn, you just turn,
And find the strength to just walk away

I don't need your strife for the rest of my life
The sun it still shines in my world
But through the darkness that reigns down on you
You've turned to being spiteful and cold

Then comes the day, a breeze blows your way
And you just turn, you just turn,
And find the strength to just walk away

A Schooner named Susan

When the sawgrass turns golden, and heavy with dew
I walk through these foothills, thinking of you
And wonder just where, your life has gone
You were my first love and it still feels so strong.

I heard that he died at some tragic end
Black ice, a snow bank, then your life changed
I wanted to come and help see you through
But I was far out at sea, forgetting about you

Time has slipped by, for so many years
But still, I remember all of your fears
Not to commit to an eternity of time
A free-spirit girl whose light had to shine.

I've sailed through these islands for so many years
I know every port and safe harbor it seems
But the one thing that always reminds me of you
The name for this schooner had to be you.

A proud little schooner fair hulled and true
Under spinnaker or storm jib she always came through
And anchored at harbor on warm stary nights
I can still feel your spirit holding me tight.

I moved back to land not too long ago
I live in the desert, waiting to grow old
But in my silent moments, with nothing to do
I dream of the time, that I had with you.

My Friend Joe

I met Joe at the factory, first week I was there
He showed me all around the place, he really seemed to care
He always had a kind word, for everyone he met
He told me once he has a life, without a regret.

I watched old Joe through the years, as we both grew old
But that smile was always there, he showed his gentle soul
Through the years we both grew old, products of our time
We were once the contenders, now we're past our prime

Old Joe was always there, with a smile and being kind
I have been retired now, almost 15 years in time
I saw it in the paper, Joe had passed away
All those kind heart memories, came flooding over me,

I went to see my old friend off, he was the man I want to be
It is the least that I could do, a kind soul looked out for me,
Rain was hanging in the air; the sky was overcast and grey
Seemed like the perfect day, to send my friend away

Minister looked at his watch, then began to pray
He wanted to be somewhere else, but here he had to stay
I looked down at the coffin, lying in the ground
One thing that hit me hard, I was standing there alone

He never had a family, his friends were somewhere else
And the final sendoff was, just me and a man of God
How can you live your life, and give yourself away
Only just to die alone, and be put down in a grave

There must be more than gratitude, to save a lonely soul
He filled his life with kindness, he grew old and died alone
There must be more than gratitude, to save a lonely soul
He filled his life with kindness, he grew old and died alone.

Sailor's life

Just caught sight of Southport light, hard abeam Goat Island
Tonight, I set my anchor down, in a Boothbay Harbor town.
Slipped the lines from Browns Wharf,
On a high tide with the sunrise
Six-day run with the gulf stream ride,
And Maine becomes my home

Nassau town was good to me, Had many nights of splendor
But she just grew tired of the inner me,
A hermit on the water.
When a sailor slips away, And heads for flat horizons
He leaves behind some circumstance,
And never will he fault her

Her golden hair and soft skin glows,
With the morning sunlight
I never could get used to it, goodbyes feel so cold
She wanted more than I could give, A hermit on the water
And as the sun set down on Nassau town,
Green Door Inn became her home

Living in the Present

Between the planning of the future,
And the pain of past regret
Lives the essence of the present,
In a place you can't forget
In the here and now,
Like the song upon the wind
It will tell you everything
And you let it sing
And understand the moment,
That you are living in

In the moment of the present,
Where truth rings in a song
You hold the essence of the moment,
And nothing can go wrong.
If you hold it true,
Your actions see it through
Mindfulness will guide you,
To the spirit of the soul
And you live within the stillness,
Where wisdom starts to grow

Living in the here and now,
Is a constant place to be
But the memories of my past mistakes,
Keep me from being clear
The inner light that guides us all,
Keeps calling out to me
And the siren calls of gratitude,
Is where we all should be

We find our own adventures
In our quest for inner peace
And the holy roller of the soul
Is calling out to me
I will not be swayed by the daily clutter,
Or the situations that do call
That is set to keep me from being free,
As others start to fall

Sometimes when I travel,
I feel like another man
I do just what I feel is right
And help out when I can
It's the gratitude and solitude
And ride the train alone
And living in the moment
It is the master's siren call

I was down at the Mermaid Garden Café

I was down at the Mermaid Café, before the noonday rush
I heard someone call out to me, in a solemn quiet hush
I know what you did she said, I know what you've done
Hiding in your solitude, it's how the hard jobs' won

Living in a mill town, that was past its prime
Looking for solutions, to the changing times
Present day America, full of hate and fear
Hoping you don't tread on me, or ever get too near

I know what you did she said, I know what you've done
Hiding in your solitude, it's not for everyone
Facing the solution, means staying on the run.

The Basin it was dying, algae on the bloom
Ranchers and the farmers, ignored the problem too
The solution to a problem, is always close at hand
The truth will be your judge, it's why you take your stand

Take the issue farther up, there is someone you should know
Inside the halls of justice, where the band aid money flows.
When the feds threw up their heads, solstice came around
Nature it was crying, and no one spoke a sound

I know what you did she said, I know what you've done
Hiding in your solitude, it's how the hard jobs done
The issue that important, you had to pack a gun.

Federalies came to town, check book in their hand
Making friends with everyone, touting future plans
Handing over mega bucks, that's how you get it done
Overpriced solutions, and greed will never run

I know what you did she said, I know what you've done
Hiding in your solitude, it's not for everyone
I know what you did she said, I know what you've done
The issue that important, you had to pack a gun.

Sometimes

Sometimes when dawn comes late, before the morning dew
I like to take a walk alone, just to think things through
I never could understand, and never could explain
The personality of the fool, and how he resists change.

Profit margins getting small, anger on the rise
Some of the hand to mouth crowd, think they can't get by.
If we can't adapt, or will not change, our ticket has arrived
Then with all the flat earth fools, we never will survive

It's times like these that test your fate, wherever you reside
The planet is getting smaller, it's time you must decide
To battle all the multitudes, or cut loose to the hills
The air is always fresher there, and where time stands still

Away from all the multitudes, where the pulse of life resides
Listen to the wilderness, and let it ring inside
A pull so strong is telling you, just where you must belong
That voice inside the wilderness, makes every fiber strong

Preplan for the good times, forget the scrape-by days
Just make sure you know the score, if it goes away
Way beyond the loneliness, at the edge of hushed despair
Cabin fever is very real, and leaves a scar in there

You stayed too long, and the money ran dry
You sit alone and wonder, will you get by
Now winter's closing in, and the candle it grows dim
The old man in the wilderness, that's my soul within.

Casper's Song

I shed a silent tear today
For a man I've never met
Just got word his son had died
My heart poured out regret

No one should ever know
The death of a family soul
From the younger generation
That never will grow old

Console your-self with memories
And show your family strength
One day there is a future dawn
When you will meet again.

I shed a silent tear today
No one saw it fall
Somehow, we can still relate
To the sadness of it all

Freelance Opportunist

Just a freelance opportunist, on the road to Montreal
Got sidetracked by the weather, and the siren call
The pulse of a little adventure, it hides within us all.
If you settle in a hillbilly camp, then the mission it is stalled.

There is a sense of freedom, when you travel on your own
Opportunities roll past your gate, not time for coming home
And when the time to travel comes, it's always in the stars
You head south in the dead of night, no one sees the scars

Bare your soul to someone, someone that you trust
Or live alone and muster, the talents that you must.
Taken at face value, it just a token jest
The side hustle of the masses, is get all you can get

I've made my peace with everyone, or some past regret
That creeps into my world, wish I could forget
But adventures of the future, take over where I am
Like a holy roller on a mission, you will not see me again

Mother Nature has a Plan

From the high desert of Oregon, to the Costa Rican shore
I've seen what man has done to the place he calls his home
The fish are gone, the lake is dead, but still no compromise
With the high desert ranchers, and all their pesticide

We once had a planet, where we all could survive
Now we are thinking twice, if we can make it out alive.
Mother nature has a plan, to spin this planet without man
And if we don't pay attention here, the shit will hit the fan.

Deep in foreign solitude, on a shore that no one knew
Costa Rica has a place, that has been visited by few
Walking on the sandy shore the high tide line of shame
A thousand pieces of plastic, all without a name.

The flat earth fools and power mongers, making all the rules
To tear down wildlife habitat, for the greed of human fools
Animals they run and hide, whenever we come near
Disappearing species, that's something we should fear

The unseen overseer, since time first had its start
Is always somewhere near, this earth it has a heart
Mother nature has a plan, to spin this planet without man
And if we don't pay attention here, the shit will hit the fan.

Phaedrus

Thought I'd go sailing, just to loosen my vibe,
I've been way to wound up, trying to survive
So, in the pre-dawn when the air's light and thin,
I slipped off the bow line to let it begin

Out of the harbor with the jib points to the wind,
And a halyard line back in my hands once again
As the bell buoy sings the change of the tide
I ride my white horse and the waves in its stride

Study the chart, then set your course true
The tide and the current will lead you on through
The compass rose knows the set and the drift
Then sail through your life, like you've never been missed.

Mair's tails are dancing across the blue sky
Telling of a weather, with seas that will run high
Soon it will storm, but the wind it is just right
To make a safe harbor, before the dark of night

A sailor will always, hold close to his heart
A love for the sea, and renegade cohorts
Brawny and ballsey, in a loose harbor town
But far out at sea, the winds calm you down

I travel through life, like I'm way out at sea
And watching for mare's tails, in the people I meet
Plan your next move, like you have nothing to fear
When the tide turns, you'll know where to steer

Boys Town Anthem

(Ballad for a New Adult)

The early years they guide you, on how to hold your ground
But under all the noise, there is something in the sound
Of a peace of mind that guides you, and leads you to a test
Hold on to your integrity, then try your very best.

Here's to those new adults, for the first time in their lives
Can do just what they want, without some adult jive.
Make your decisions wisely, you need to build your tribe
If you don't look out for someone else, they pick up that vibe

Ride the wave before you, or take a single stand
Whatever you do, do with heart and head and hand
Take the safest journey, or ride on a gambler's thought
Just give back to everyone, enough to tie the knot

Build your friendships wisely, they will influence your life
Honesty is nothing more, than trusting you are right.
There is someone in your future, that needs all your respect
Treat everyone with kindness, and wait for the consequence

If we've never failed, we never tried, to conquer a new world
But honesty and integrity, are the values we must hold.
Some are born for greatness, some are born to serve
We are all born for a purpose, that has not been exposed.

One small action that helped someone, will never be ignored
When someone in your future, wants to come on board
The favors of a friend, will always help you through
Build your friendships like a fortress, and share the inner you

From this moment forward, one thing you must protect
That little seed of knowledge, behind your self-respect
Every thought, action, and deed, one thing you must protect
That little seed of knowledge, behind your self-respect

A Sailor's Song

Just caught sight of Southport light, hard a-beam Goat Island
Tonight, I'll let the anchor sway, in a Boothbay Harbor town

The evening sunlight fills her face, golden hair around her
She is the silent siren call, of this quiet harbor town
I never did get to know, her everlasting humor
Don't expect a wanderer to ever settle down.

Just caught sight of Nassau light, ride the slack tide dockside
Drinking up, Green Door Pub, Browns wharf on the landline,

A six-day run with the wind, puts me in the Leeward's
I'd rather live on a sailing boat, than live a life on shore
But no one has the adventure gene, that I have in me
Maybe I'll go to Monserrat, hook up an island girl

Beam reach to the Dutch West Indies, where all trade begins
Front street in St Marten, its where I like to stay
Taste the island flavors and be who you should be
Watch out for the siren call, they leave you weak and lonely

Midnight boat to a back cove haunt, feeling like a pirate
Crocus Bay on the British Isle, think I'll stay a while
Island girls so uptight, tourists' easy pickings
I hide out in a hidden cove with future thoughts that roam

Once in a While

Once in a while, I turn to you, and breath a gentle sigh
As a sea of calm enters me, with a vision on my mind
And you look at me and understand, just what it is I know
Then for one brief instant, we have a common goal

Once in a while I understand, why I wear this mask
Speak the truth for the common good, is not an easy task
Opinion's rule, with the vengeance of a storm-tossed sea
And the anguish of doing it alone, not all it's meant up to be

Deep within the secret chamber, where we always fear to go
There holds a secret vision, that our thoughts do first unfold
The inner dream of what will be, is never far from you
It's only inner prejudice, that keeps you from your goal

Understand the inner you, and follow your inner goal
Just realize the empty pain, of acting all alone
No one cares just where you are, or where you want to be
But only you will understand, the goal of tranquility.

A martyr cries out in the night, from the pain and inner strife
Why does he anguish all alone, when no one is in his sight?
Then stands up tall before first light, and aims his arrow true
Deep into humanity's soul, to expose the inner truth.

Iron Horse of Solitude

Sometimes in the morning, when words get in the way
A gentle breeze of knowledge, seems to come your way
Then a change in life occurs, I head for the deep unknown
Because I've found my iron horse and ride road alone

I could've sold my mind to the cable box, sitting in my chair
I could've sat at home all day, on the dole and drinking beer
But I got no wife, got no life, I got to get me out of here
The iron horse of solitude gives me purpose for being here

The iron horse of solitude, takes you down the road
To another state or place in time, something you must do
I just left Wisconsin, heading for the Dixie line
I've got 40 feet of produce, and a deadline on my mind

Next week I'll be in Kansas, if the weather it holds tight
Spending time, watching miles, drive on through the night
I found a place on the Texas coast, I'd kinda like to go
I can walk the beach alone and for one day call it home

I used to have it all, but my wife she died too young
Left me with the burden, to raise our only son
He's gone to a distant town, got a wife and settled down
And I just like to be alone, friendships have gone cold

I shake my head in vain disgust, at the attitudes I see
But in the iron horse of solitude, it's where I want to be
Watching out on the prairie sky, letting the miles roll by
And knowing I can do some good, before I say goodbye

Travels

I've always liked to travel,
I've always liked to roam
But the highway can be lonely,
when it is your only home

I once lived in along the coast
of sometimes foggy Maine
I watched the Osprey on their nest
and listen to the loons at play
In quiet times I often dream,
of going back one day.

I once lived in North Carolina,
would not go back again
Black man treated like dirt down there,
white boys are the Klan
Water Moccasins hang in trees,
to scare the fishermen.

I've always liked to travel,
I've always liked to roam
But the highway can be lonely,
when it is your only home

I once lived in Florida
it's very muggy there
The sun it shines down every day
for almost the whole year

But when those big green clouds roll in,
get your ass out of there

I spent one night in Georgia
really had a scare
Not too fond of strangers,
if you travel there
Got a tire iron across my back,
for wearing my long hair

I travelled once through Texas,
they have big hearts down there
Will help an honest stranger
but best you beware
A Texan is like a hornet,
and can sting you if you dare

California that was fun,
with their veggie attitudes
All peace and love and cyber stuff
but what gave me the blues
That scuzzy old rancher down the street,
just sold for a million two.

I've always liked to travel,
I've always liked to roam
But the highway can be lonely,
when it is your only home

I sailed the Caribbean,
skipper for the crew
We fished and drank
and ate all day
We were modern pirates,
all Jolly Roger's too

I packed a gun in Oregon,
kept it on my hip
Had a hot load in the chamber,
in case some local flipped
They're just not strong on education,
or left-wing points of view

Now Arizona is my view,
like many years ago
Retired now and all kicked back,
with a peaceful attitude
Where water sports, and gentle walks,
refresh the quiet mood.

I've always liked to travel,
I've always liked to roam
But the highway can be lonely,
when it is your only home

Miguel

He grew up in Nicaragua,
the street was all he knew
His father died when he was ten,
but his mother saw him through
He studied hard and learned to read,
his friends all ran the streets
Because he had dreams to fill,
and held hard to his beliefs

One day when he was walking home,
a voice called out his name
He turned to see a glowing light,
and an angel showed his face
Was this some kind of dream,
or just some faint embrace
In the higher realm of inner change,
he always knew he had a place

Miguel called out and said,
show me what I must do
There must be more to my life,
then just a ghetto fool
But the silence then was broken,
by a turf war in the streets
He ran and hid behind the trees,
then he found his inner peace

I must make my life complete,
and become some holy man
Like a Buddha of the Latin world,
I must not live in strife
To stop this turf war violence,
and try and take a stand
But when he got home, a ricochet,
had destroyed his mother life.

He spent three long days in silence,
and searched his inner soul
Why must I live this way,
until I'm spent and old
My life down here is worthless,
where violence takes its toll
The only way to change this world,
is up in the land of gold

He packed a bag and headed north,
as the monsoons cleared the skies
Fifteen days on a desert trail,
with a freedom in his eyes
The boarder was the obstacle,
that no one could revive
But coyotes do the boarder run,
if you pay for the midnight ride

From Nogales down to Naco,
coyotes wait their turn
To take your money for a midnight ride,
to the land of the golden road
Put aside your fear,
and try to hang on to the ride
Run the streets, and get wet feet,
just to reach the other side

Shots ring out, and one goes down,
when the time to cross has come
But Miguel and the others,
are now in a full-on run
They reach the other side
and walk-up unknown streets
No one seems to notice,
that they all have the same wet feet.

They separate and go their ways,
use the desert as a hide
Always on the lookout for,
white trucks a green stipe on the side
He reaches the inner city,
and hopes to find some rest
But no one here really cares,
and put's him to the test

His life is now of servitude,
a day job to survive
Labor jobs in the relentless sun,
a way to stay alive
He knows he will never make it,
from his ghetto strife
But now he can sleep at night,
with the dreams of a better life

Not wanting to draw suspicion
he hides inside himself
One day he will reach his goal,
of a family and wife
But for now, the day job market,
helps him stay alive
As he keeps his dreams and aspirations,
all locked up inside

When you Step Inside my Room

You're standing there with open arms, smile upon your face
But your true intent for me, is another dreamed disgrace
If you could see inside yourself, you would understand
The image you project at me, is just a slight of hand

If you cannot be honest with yourself beyond your worth
How do you expect me, to stand up to my curse
I am a lonely sailor, that has been storm tossed at sea
And you are not the safe harbor, that you claim to be

If you could only see, the crippled soul within
You would have compassion, and know where to begin
To add some inner strength to me, instead of tear me down
Because you are just another circus, just another clown

Like the carnival that is your life, forever on the roll
That only wants a piece of me for some end game goal
You have no inner passion; you have no point of rule
You just want a piece of me, to make me be the fool

I find my perfect bliss, is shattered in the dust
When you walk into the room and hand me all your trust
Like some smiling conversation it leads to the road of greed
Understand the real you, it's hiding behind your needs

And the song that is the moment silently turns to gloom
It's the inner song that follows you, you step inside a room
You cannot hide the atmosphere, you cannot hide the vibe
It is whatever is on your mind, you're planning for this time

The Legend Lives on

Somewhere past the border, In the Windward Island chain
Near the edge of another time, I heard a man exclaim
You never will belong here, your skin it fights the sun
You are just another expat, your soul was born to run

I could not help but wonder, at his sense of latitude
Living in a Savana hut, how he viewed the world
He seemed to read right through me, a window to my soul
As if he'd always known me, a brother of his own

He told me of the present, he spoke of days of old
He told me of the future, then he spoke of pirate's gold
It's been in my blood for many years, and my grandpas' too
Chasing after pirates' gold, and playing the game of fools

I sailed away on the rising tide, bound for Dominic
To the place he told me of, my pirates gold to seek
Now I've found my pirates gold, it's bounty I can't spend
It lives inside this island girl, and the heart of her Carib kin

I said Goodbye to a Daughter

I was somewhere in the Rockies, Kootenays are my friends
I always go back there, when life gives me the bends
I said goodbye to a daughter, that I never had
She thought that I owed her, for things she should have had

I had to leave her far behind, when she was growing up
Her mother she had lied to me, about the freedoms I give up
What sort of life long plans begins with telling lies?
Bring someone to America, and rip its freedom from my eyes

Have you ever trusted, promises and vows?
Only to watch them shatter, scattered in the dust
Then watch the manipulation, as freedom's line was crossed
Bring someone to America, just to be their boss

She never will understand, the pain that she has caused
Just by being selfish, that has always been her cause
If you ever see her, tell her thanks a lot
A daughter has a special gift, for tearing out your heart.

Chapter 2

Political Winds

Private Carter passed away

Private Carter passed away, just before Thanksgiving Day
Lying frozen in the snow, homeless shelter, it was closed

He learned to fight while overseas, came back to his destiny
Did not want anyone to see, a demon soul that he could be
Travelled roads and railway yards, hoping on a distant star
He could feel emotions one more time

Klamath Falls in Oregon, the winter's short the summer long
But last year they got it wrong, high desert storm raged on
A Foot of snow came down, nothing moved except someone
Looking for some place to hide, and shelter from the storm.

Homeless shelter just in sight, no lights on, it's just not right
Sudden fear grips him tight, sign said closed no help tonight.
How could they not see, this upcoming travesty?
Winds will howl all night, hears God call him home tonight

Saw a schoolyard just nearby, that is where he went to die
They found him in the early light, he was gone into the night
. Never to be warm again, they never gave him anything.
How could this happen in my town,
We didn't see this going down.

Budget flaws and attitudes, had no funds for getting through
This winter storm before it's time, November is harvest time
But this year a storm came through, inaction caused us to
Give another tortured soul his final resting home

I swear to God you cannot see, just how fragile life can be
Until you find your life unwound,
On some cardboard on the ground.

Private Carter passed away, just before Thanksgiving Day
Lying frozen in the snow, homeless shelter, it was closed
I swear to God you cannot see, just how fragile life can be
Until you find yourself unwound,
And lay your head on cardboard on the ground.

There's a Target on my Back

There is a target on my back
I can feel it in this room
Standing back behind me,
Their face all full of gloom

Sorry you do not understand
What it is I say and do
I take you through the looking glass,
To see the inner you.

Standing for ecology
And try to improve our life
Is not some left-wing looney trick
To complicate or strife
It is just the soul of inner man
That speaks for what is right

The new Russian War

One day your setting fenceposts, in the hot Oregon sun
Next day your riding shotgun, the antififaz's coming to town
Bruno's got the A-K, Sally's got the Glock
Got to protect the city, from that violent left-wing mob

Facebook trending violence, twitter lights up too
A hundred unknown people, wanting to get through
Dialog is happening, on cell phones far and wide
Read the latest text, just to stay alive.

No one was really coming; it looks like you got played
And the streets of our city are peaceful once again
Trending on the internet, who the hell was that
Pushing all the buttons, to provoke some ground attack

Deep within some foreign room, where the internet prevails
Are a hundred Russian Soldiers, creating Facebook tales
With every fear attainable, to the left and to the right
The new front of the Russian war, the internet of life.

Turn off the net and stand up tall
Look me in the eye, and show your soul
I do not care about your politics; opinions make me gag.
Taking care of business, it's the breeze that waves the flag.

I don't care about your politics, opinions make me gag
It's the art of the honest business deal,
That's the breeze that waves my flag.

Something on the Radio

Something on the radio, does not fit quite right
Someone talking shit, about my way of life
Personal Philosophies winds us up too tight
And if you try and change my view, you may not get it right.

Anger is the vibe today, hate talk radio getting old
Destroys a country before you realize, what was sold
Who pays for all that hate talk stuff, from a talk show host?
Anyone with common sense, would find it very old.

But when personal ambition, has been worn too thin
Diet's not right, clothes too tight, thinking you can win
So, you sit around and mope all day, and listen to the radio
About everything that's wrong, with another point of view

Children in another land, work into the night
Homework and assignments, they have to get it right
Elsewhere in another land, plans and dreams unfold
About their latest product or a factory to build

Deep within America, another point of view
Sit around in anger, hatred on the stew
White trash hate is showing through, they come into light
Then you become the target, for doing what is right

The Grey Clouds of Winter

I once met a man, on some far island home
He claimed he travelled, the world on his own
A clairvoyant savant, with a future he told
Of power and treason, about to unfold.

When the grey clouds of winter, have left the noon sky
And the Snow Geese have gone, to their home by the bay
In the future of spring, when all dreams come true
There lies a dark cloud, and the target is you.

When an oak leaf's as big, as a chipmunk's ear
The Amish claim, that planting is near
But what is that wind, that blows fridgetly cold
A cold icy drama, about to unfold.

I once met a man, on some far island home
He claimed he travelled, the world on his own
A clairvoyant savant, with a future he told
Of power and treason, about to unfold.

He turned and he said, without even a smile
The death of the country, takes a short while
The blind grab for power, is the virus within
If you can't see it coming, you never will win.

Anger at the moment, cannot be denied
When emotions take over, the political tide
They don't see it coming, or cannot behold
That a nation in peril, is about to unfold

It's there in our history, it's there in our past
From Boston Harbor, to Bay of Pigs bash
Misguided fools, cause the havoc you've seen
Used like dumb pawns, to wipe the slate clean.

And hiding in the corner, far behind your view
The master of the con, is coming just for you
As the voice of sound reason, disappears from view
A country falls, and the vision is through.

Lemon Frosting

Lemon frosting starts to melt, every time she thinks of me
Obviously, she does not agree with the likes of me
Lemon frosting starts to melt, she needs a sugar treat
Someone who will talk to her about how she disagrees
She hangs with all the super-rich, like she is one of those
With a name badge on her chest, keeps her at their toes

Do not tell anyone, because they will all see
She does not like those immigrants, that talk political beats
You're from another country, and you were taught in school
The only thing that matters, is trust in the golden rule
But she grew up in America and has the only right
To talk a political vibe, because she alone is right.

I Don't Care What You Say or You Think

I don't care what you say or you think
Your attitude tells me your still on the brink
Of a fantasy dance where the devils in charge
Drooling for power, and acting out large

I don't care if you think that it's right
It's a nation in peril if you turn out the light
Why do you think that, the man at the rails
Is no more than a mob boss, in tux and in tails

Character matters, was thrown to the wolves
It's all about power, and who follows fools
Ditching honest integrity, that we all expect
You lie cheat and steal, for the power it gets

What were the values, at this countries birth?
Are we nothing but anger, deposed of our worth?
How do you sleep with yourself in the night?
When you cheated someone, and then turned out their light

It's the man at the helm, that needs to hold true
To the values inside us, we're all living through
How can we dream of a future in store?
If we stop the truth, outside our front door

We all have a fire that burns in our soul
If we use it for hate, it's nobody's rule
Why would you think I could never be told
To live in the shadows till I grow old

You make the choice of who gets to stay
Ethics and standards need a fair play
And the king of the con, is not the right choice
For a country that needs to set its own course.

The bearded hold mass for the king of the con
Had fools for parents and now they are grown
To be nothing but bearded hateful and scorned
Unable to know the truth from the con

The bottom line comes at the end of the day
What have you done for your world in a way?
That shows that your purpose for being right here
Is to just blow smoke and suck up my air

The world of the con, is to never give up
On some strange notion that follows the script
Laid out in the silence of some darkened crypt
That buries the truth and feeds us all shit

The silent majority stands at the gate
Respecting the leaders devoid of this hate
Where laws are developed by our chosen few
And the womb of democracy glows in their soul

I don't care what you think that is right
It's a nation in peril if you turn out the light
Why do you think that the man at the rails
Is no more than a mob boss in tux and in tails

I don't care what you say or you think
Your attitude tells me your still on the brink
Of a fantasy dance where the devils in charge
Drooling for power, and acting out large

Black Lives Matter

The white kids from the suburbs,
marching in the street
Screaming black lives matter,
like that some kind of treat
While the black guy from the hood
just tries to make ends meet
Got no job, the school was broke,
he hardly learned to read
To rise out of that poverty,
and make a life fulfilled
Takes more guts than shruburb larva
yelling for a thrill.
You try being black
and go searching for a job
Between the crackheads, welfare moms,
a beat cop stares you down.
Substandard wage, substandard job,
but at least it pays the rent
No time left for dreaming,
that money's all been spent
Just trying to make it to the end of day,
and survive a ghetto night
With loves emotion tucked inside
afraid to show its light.

Then one day you bend the law,
and of course, you try and run
But the blue line says- you come with me
and reaches for his gun
Not knowing you're an honest man
he starts to aim at you
Now before you decide to run,
you better think this through
Your word is golden inside the court,
no judge will be diss to you
But if you run, you're going to get,
what they call a through and through
A cap in the ass if you're riding on luck,
if not code F, dead duck
But the martyrs of the street scene
cry until they're blue.

The martyrs of the street scene,
don't know what you've been through
The martyrs of the street scene,
do not have a clue

Chapter 3

The Poets Society

And you say the battle is over

And you say that the battle is over
And finally, the war is all done
Go tell it to those with the wind in their nose
Who run from the sound of the gun

And write it on the sides
Of the great whaling ships
Or on ice floes where conscience is tossed
With the wild in their eyes
It is they who must die and
It's we who must measure the loss

And you say that the battle is over
And finally, the world is at peace
You mean no one is dying
and mothers don't weep
or it's not in the papers at least.
There are those who would deal
in the darkness of life
There are those who would
tear down the sun.
And most men are ruthless
but some will still weep,
When the gifts we were given are gone.

Now the blame cannot fall
on the heads of a few.
It's become such a part of the race
It's eternally tragic,
that which is magic,
be killed at the end of the glorious chase.
From young seals to great whales,
from waters to wood
They will fall just like weeds in the wind.
With fur coats and perfumes
and trophies on walls,
what a hell of a race to call men.

With the wild in their eyes
It is they who must die
And it's we who must measure the loss

-   **Dave Mallett**

I heard your voice in the wind today

I heard your voice in the wind today
And I turned to see your face
The warmth of that wind caressed me
As I stood so silently in place

I felt your touch of the sun today
As the warmth filled the sky
I closed my eyes for your embrace
And my spirit soured so high

I saw your eyes in the window pane
As I watched the falling rain
It seemed as each raindrop fell
It quietly said your name

I held you in my heart today
It made me feel complete
You may have died, but you're not gone
You're always a part of me

As long as the sun does shine
The wind does blow and the rain does fall
You will live on inside of me forever
For that is all that my heart knows

-    *Unknown*

Little Bird

Little bird come sit upon my window sill
Sat there through the falling rain
I watched that little bird upon my window sill
Saw my thoughts of you go by again
Picture of my face on the window pane
Is it tears I see or is it rain?

Yeah, I remember how we talked before we said goodbye
Too young to know this world outside our door
And how we laughed and said our love was free
Like birds that fly the winds
Well the rainy day made me think of you once more

I have no regrets about the past, I see how young we were
When our world was love and life was but a thought
Many things go many ways and many times but once
Well our lives have passed and that love is but a thought
Picture of my face, on the window pane
Is it tears I see or is it rain?

So as the thoughts go tumbling back I wonder how you loved
Wonder if you've seen that little bird
I wonder if he's sat upon your windowsill
I wonder if you'll ever hear these words
And the picture of my face, on the window pane
Is it tears I see or is it rain?

- *Jerry Jeff Walker*

Night Guard

Forty-four's no age to start again
But the bulls were getting tough and was never free of pain
Where others blew their winnings getting tanked
Most of his got banked saving for the farm
He never thought she'd wait for him at all
She wanted more than broken bones, trophies on the wall
But when he quit and finally got the farm
She ran into his arms and now they've got a kid

He was star of all the rodeos but now they rob him blind
It took eighteen years of Brahma bulls and life on the line
To get this spread and a decent herd
But now he spends his time pulling night guard

He told her that he'd got it for the game
A "Winnie" 303 with his initials on the frame
Riding in the scabbard at his knee. Tonight he's gonna see
Who's getting all the stock
Seventh one this summer yesterday
Half a year of profits gone, and now there's hell to pay
The cops say they know who, but there's no proof
The banker hit the roof, and damn near took the car

He was star of all the rodeos but now they rob him blind
It took eighteen years of Brahma bulls and life on the line
To get this spread and a decent herd
But now he spends his time pulling night guard

He hears the wire popping by the road
Sees the blacked out Reo coming for another load
This time, it's not one they take but two
Two minutes and they're through, and laughing in the cab
And here'll be the end of this tonight
Cause all the proof he needs is lying steady in his sights
It may be just the worst thing he could do
But he squeezes off a few, then make his call to town

He was star of all the rodeos but now they rob him blind
It took eighteen years of Brahma bulls and life on the line
To get this spread and a decent herd
But now he's doing time pulling night guard....

-   ***Stan Rodgers***

Pour the Gold

Pour the gold into the hold

Take it out to sea
Hungry mouths are waiting
Outside the granary

Oh, I've slept into your chilly mornings
Awoken by the dew
I've worked to help a harvest
Now I want to see it through.

Won't you meet me by the harbor
If we make it through the mountains
What a journey it would be
To the boat that lies so still.

- *Cedric Smith*

Raven In the Storm

I'm the latest apparition
Cutting slices in the night
I come through without permission
Moving in and out of human sight

I'm the tapping on your shoulder
I'm the raven in the storm
I'll take shelter in your rafters
I'm the shiver when you're warm

I'm the gold in California
I'm the well in Mexico
Like the vultures in the valley
I will wait for you to go

I'm the gypsy in your pocket
I'm the horseman in your dreams
I'm the reason dogs are barking
I'm the hand that stops the scream

I'm the baby's cry that isn't
I am the distant relative
I'm the scratching in the ceiling
I'm advice you shouldn't give

I'm the ghost of a traveling salesman
My foot will be there in your door
Though I can walk through walls and windows
I will knock just like before

I'm the darkness in your daughter
I'm the spot beneath the skin
I'm the scarlet on the pavement
I am the broken heart within

I won't take a train to nowhere
I will not touch just anyone
Ask a stranger why I'm waiting
In the chamber of a gun

- *John Gorka and Geoff Bartley*

Renaissance Waltz

I like the way that your hair falls away
When the night brings a candle to you
And I like to stare as you come down the stair
And the light from the landing shines through
And how many fallen leaves will it take to believe
That autumn has finally come
The weathers grown colder and we've both grown older
It's hard to believe we're still one
Let's dance that old dance once more,
Still move as smooth on that old ballroom floor
I'll wear my Sunday best, you wear your favorite dress
Lock up the door, and let's dance that old dance once more

You hung around keep my feet on the ground
When I acted as proud as a fool
We were kids and we've grown, we've got kids of our own
Got to raise by the old golden rule
Somehow it seems, some of our dreams
Got discarded somewhere on the road
When all that was true could be found in the blue
Of your eyes that still sparkle and glow

The Frost King has come and with a flick of his thumb
Turned the windows to Renaissance art
As we sit round the fire with no need to enquire
About the ways of the soul and the heart
Years passed us by like a soft whispered sigh
Not noticing youth as it flew
It's easy to tell that you wear your age well
Not trying to prove you're still you

-   *Valdy*

Seven Spanish Angels

He looked down into her brown eyes
And said say a prayer for me
She threw her arms around him whispered
God will keep us free

They could see the riders coming
He said This is my last fight
If they take me back to Texas
They won't take me back alive

There were seven Spanish angels
At the altar of the sun
They were praying for the lovers
In the valley of the gun

When the battle stopped and the smoke cleared
There was thunder from the throne
And seven Spanish angels
Took another angel home

She reached down and picked the gun up
That lay smoking in his hand
She said Father please forgive me
I can't make it without my man

And she knew the gun was empty
And she knew she could not win
But her final prayer was answered
When the rifles fired again

-   ***Troy Seals and Eddie Setzer***

Silent Passage

Before the war I had no need for traveling
Indeed, I do not know what made it so important to leave
And after all this time I found that I'm avoiding me
For nothing more or less then fear
Of what I have to gain from staying in the clear
All though it's only coming home that brings you near

Master Dough, my brother, is a sailor
Upon this ship of light we are the master sails in the wind
And you can understand, we need a hand to guide us in
So many claim to be the one
But like a shadow on the sun they fade and spin
And we are scattered on the ocean once again

Before the war I had no need for traveling
Indeed, I do not know what made it so important to leave
And after all this time I found that I'm avoiding me
For nothing more or less then fear
Of what I have to gain from staying in the clear
Although it's only coming home that brings you near
Although it's only coming home that brings the tears

-   *Bob Carpenter*

Star in the Black Sky Shining

There was a woman I saw on the street,
I swear she was wearing the moon on her feet.
She said, "Do you know me?" and I said, "I don't know."
She told me to listen, and then I could go.

And there was a boy who I found on the road,
I said, "Are you lost, with nowhere to go?"
And he said, "No I'm not, I believe that you are."
And he told me to sit, on the hood of the car.

He said, "I am the course that the river is winding,
And I am the horse that the angel is riding,
And I am the source of the love you are finding.
Do you know who I am? It is blinding,
I am the star, in the black sky shining."

There was a dog, who had followed me home,
He was not young, but not fully grown.
And he said, "Do you know me? we spoke on the phone,
I was a king, and the world is my throne."

He said, "I am the flame, in the heat of the fire,
And I am to blame, for the tongue of the liar,
And I am the same, as the birds on the wire.
Do you know who I am? it is blinding,
I am the star, in the black sky shining."

And there was a thief who was tied to a pole,
At his feet was a list, of the things that he stole.
And I said, "I am only playing a role."
And he asked if I dared, look deep in his soul.

He said, I am the heart of the warrior child,
And I am the moment, that the beast becomes mild,
And I am the part, of the soul that is wild.
Do you know who I am? It is blinding,
I am the star, in the black sky shining, oh.

And I come from the light, it is blinding,
For I am the star, in the black sky shining, oh.

-   ***John Stewart***

The Believer

I can't imagine, that's my problem
I'm searching always for better weather
The coast is rough and the tide is running
I chase my shadow till I remember

The fine and free days have gone to storming
I spend my time with joy and sorrow
But one is dying and one is crying
I may not be around tomorrow

My dearest friends are total strangers
I call them heroes; they call me lonely
I wish them wisdom and self-destruction
And hope someday they'll come to know me

The forest grows around my door now
But I am dreaming of a meadow
Where I may lie in frosty sunlight
Far between the earth a stray shadow

Though I'm not a God for certain
There are steps we all must follow
He's a beggar and a king
He's a falcon and a swallow

-   *Bob Carpenter*

The Mary Ellen Carter

She went down last October
in a pouring driving rain
The skipper he'd been drinking
and the Mate he felt no pain
Too close to Three Mile Rock,
and she was dealt her mortal blow
And the Mary Ellen Carter settled low

There were just us five aboard her
when she finally was awash
We'd worked like hell to save her –
all heedless of the cost
And the groan she gave as she went down
it caused us to proclaim
That the Mary Ellen Carter would rise again

Well the owners wrote her off;
not a nickel would they spend.
She gave twenty years of service boys
then met her sorry end
But insurance paid the loss to us,
they let her rest below
Then they laughed at us
and said we had to go

But we talked of her all winter,
some days around the clock
For she's worth a quarter million,
afloat and at the dock
And with every jar that hit the bar,
we swore we would remain
And make the Mary Ellen Carter rise again

Rise again ---- rise again ---
that her name not be lost
To the knowledge of men
Those who loved her best
-and were with her till the end
Will make the Mary Ellen Carter rise again

All spring now we've been with her
on a barge lent by a friend
Three dives a day in hard hat suit
and twice I've had the bends
Thank God it's only sixty feet
and the currents here are slow
Or I'd never have the strength to go below

We've patched her rents, stopped her vents
dogged hatch & porthole down
Put cables to her 'fore and aft'
and girded her around
Tomorrow noon we hit the air and then take up the strain
And make the Mary Ellen Carter rise again

Rise again ---- rise again --- that her name not be lost
To the knowledge of men
Those who loved her best -and were with her till the end
Will make the Mary Ellen Carter rise again

For we couldn't leave her there,
you see to crumble into scale
She'd saved our lives so many times,
living through the gale
And the laughing, drunken rats
who left her to a sorry grave
They won't be laughing in another day

And you to whom adversity
has dealt the final blow
With smiling bastards lying to you
everywhere you go
Turn to and put out all your strength
of arm and heart and brain
And like the Mary Ellen Carter, rise again

Rise again --- rise again – though your heart it be broken
And life about to end
No matter what you've lost, be it a home, a love, a friend
Like the Mary Ellen Carter, rise again ...

-   *Stan Rogers*

About The Author

The author is the umpteenth
Earl of the House of Honour,
a title of no significance that he gave up
when he became an American Citizen.
But the family spirit still drips from his soul.

Trevor David Honour   ~   The Vagabond Poet